CONFEDERATE GENERAL
STONEWALL JACKSON

by Robin S. Doak

Content Adviser: Babs Funkhouser,
Director, Stonewall Jackson Museum,
Strasburg, Virginia

Reading Adviser: Alexa L. Sandmann, Ed.D.,
Professor of Literacy, College and Graduate School
of Education, Health and Human Services,
Kent State University

Compass Point Books ✦ Minneapolis, Minnesota

Compass Point Books
151 Good Counsel Drive
P.O. Box 669
Mankato, MN 56002-0669

This book was manufactured with paper containing at least 10 percent post-consumer waste.

On the cover: General Stonewall Jackson at the Battle of First Manassas, also known as the First Battle of Bull Run

Photographs ©: The Granger Collection, New York, cover, 16, 20, 21, 26; North Wind Picture Archives, 4, 9, 12, 31, 35; The Corcoran Gallery of Art/Corbis, 5; Library of Congress, 6, 8, 11, 29, 37, 41; Virginia Military Institute Archives, 10, 15, 18, 19, 22, 34; Dallas Historical Society, Texas/The Bridgeman Art Library, 14; Private Collection/The Bridgeman Art Library, 24; Réunion des Musées Nationaux/Art Resource, N.Y., 27; Edward Owen/Art Resource, N.Y., 32; Todd Muskopf/Alamy, 39.

Editor: Sue Vander Hook
Page Production: Bobbie Nuytten
Photo Researcher: Svetlana Zhurkin
Cartographer: XNR Productions, Inc.
Library Consultant: Kathleen Baxter

Art Director: LuAnn Ascheman-Adams
Creative Director: Joe Ewest
Editorial Director: Nick Healy
Managing Editor: Catherine Neitge

Library of Congress Cataloging-in-Publication Data
Doak, Robin S. (Robin Santos), 1963–
   Confederate general: Stonewall Jackson / by Robin S. Doak; content adviser, Babs Funkhouser; reading adviser, Alexa L. Sandmann.
      p. cm. — (We the people)
Includes bibliographical references and index.
   ISBN 978-0-7565-4110-1 (library binding)
   1. Jackson, Stonewall, 1824–1863—Juvenile literature. 2. Generals—Confederate States of America—Biography—Juvenile literature. 3. Confederate States of America—Army—Biography—Juvenile literature. 4. United States—History—Civil War, 1861–1865—Campaigns—Juvenile literature. I. Funkhouser, Babs. II. Sandmann, Alexa L. III. Title.
E467.1.J15D625 2009
973.7'3092—dc22
[B]   2008037630

Visit Compass Point Books on the Internet at *www.compasspointbooks.com*
or e-mail your request to *custserv@compasspointbooks.com*

Table of Contents

"Like a Stone Wall"

The smell of gunpowder and cries of wounded men drifted across the parched battlefield near Manassas Junction, Virginia. The hot July sun beat down on Union and Confederate soldiers alike. The men had been fighting since early morning, and both sides were exhausted.

The Union expected an easy victory over the Confederate Army at the Battle of First Manassas. The North called it the First Battle of Bull Run.

It was July 21, 1861, the day of the first major battle of
the Civil War, and Union troops were winning. They had pushed
the Confederates back, and Southern soldiers were fleeing. If
the Union could win this battle,
it might bring an early end to the
Civil War.

One Confederate com-
mander, however, was not ready
to admit defeat. Colonel Thomas
Jackson refused to give up. As
Southern troops retreated, Jackson
ordered his men to remain where
they were, form a long line, and
wait for the North to attack.

Jackson's determination
gave hope to other Confederate

*Confederate General Thomas
"Stonewall" Jackson*

soldiers. General Bernard Bee saw Jackson and cried out, "Look! There is Jackson standing like a stone wall! Rally behind the

Jackson provided the determination needed for the South to win the first major battle of the Civil War.

Virginians!" Jackson led his men, yelling and shouting, in an attack on Northern soldiers, who fled the assault. By the end of the day, the South had won the Battle of First Manassas. Jackson, now simply called "Stonewall," became one of the first military heroes of the Civil War.

Problems between the North and South

had been building for years over the issues of slavery and states' rights. Disagreements were dividing the country. When Abraham Lincoln was elected president of the United States, South Carolina seceded from the Union. It no longer wanted to be part of the United States. Six other Southern states soon followed. On February 4, 1861, these seven states formed their own country—the Confederate States of America. Virginia was the next state to secede from the Union. Eventually, the Confederacy would include 11 Southern states.

Jackson was one of many Virginians who chose to remain loyal to his state, not to his country. During the two years he fought for the Confederacy, he became known as one of the greatest commanders of the Civil War. He defeated Union armies much larger than his own and turned likely Confederate defeats into victories.

Throughout the dark days of war, Jackson was a symbol of

victory and hope to Southerners. Many believed that "Stonewall" was unbeatable. Just the sight of the general on horseback caused Confederate soldiers to burst into cheers.

But Jackson's untimely death in the middle of the war would one day turn their confidence into despair.

Jackson's horse, Little Sorrel, was strong and tireless, much like Jackson himself.

2 Growing Up

Thomas Jackson was born January 21, 1824, in Clarksburg, a small frontier town in what is now West Virginia. He was the third child born to Jonathan and Julia Jackson. Jonathan was a smart, friendly attorney, but he enjoyed gambling and struggled to pay his growing family's bills. Julia was the daughter of a prosperous Virginia merchant.

Tragedy struck the Jackson family in 1826 when Thomas' sister Elizabeth died of typhoid fever. Just two weeks later, Thomas' father died of the same disease. The following day, Julia gave birth to the

Jonathan Jackson

couple's fourth child, a baby girl named Laura.

With young children to support and debts to pay, Julia couldn't make ends meet. She remarried in 1830, but her new husband didn't like her children. In 1831, Julia sent them to live with relatives. The oldest, Warren, stayed with Julia's family.

Stonewall Jackson was devoted to his sister Laura.

Seven-year-old Thomas and 5-year-old Laura moved in with their father's relatives in Jackson's Mill, now in West Virginia.

Just three months after the children left, Julia Jackson died giving birth to a son named William. The Jackson children now had no father or mother. For the next 11 years, Thomas and Laura lived with their Uncle Cummins Jackson, a well-to-do man who had worked hard to be a success. He expected the children to work hard, too. Thomas worked in his uncle's mill and tended the crops and farm animals. When he wasn't working, Thomas attended the little school that his uncle set up at the mill.

When Thomas was 16, he took his first paying job as a

As a boy, Stonewall Jackson worked at his uncle's mill, tended livestock, and harvested crops.

schoolteacher. He taught three months, earning a total of $5.64, and then took a job as the county's constable, a type of sheriff. The following year, Thomas was admitted to the U.S. Military Academy at West Point, New York. The academy trained young men to become U.S. Army officers.

Cadets were trained in artillery at the U.S. Military Academy at West Point.

Thomas had less schooling than many of the other cadets, and classes were not easy for him. At the end of his first year, he was 51st in his class of 101 cadets. Determined to do better, he studied day and night to bring up his grades, lighting a candle to read by after sunset. His hard work paid off, and Thomas rose in rank every year. By the time he graduated from West Point in the summer of 1846, he was 17th in his class of 59 cadets.

After graduation, Thomas was appointed second lieutenant in the 1st Artillery Regiment of the Army. He was excited about his first military assignment in Mexico. The United States and Mexico were at war, and the young man was certain he would see battle.

3

Army Life

*I*n October 1846, 22-year-old Thomas Jackson joined his regiment in Mexico. The United States and its southern neighbor had been at war since May, battling over the exact location of the U.S.-Mexican border. Jackson's first taste of battle came in March 1847, when U.S. troops attacked the Mexican city of Veracruz. The battle ended when the citizens of the city surrendered.

The U.S. Army held Veracruz under siege for 20 days, from March 9 to March 29, 1847; the Mexicans surrendered, and the Americans occupied the city.

The young officer quickly earned the respect and admiration of his fellow soldiers. Under fire, Jackson proved to be both brave and calm. During the Battle of Chapultepec, he convinced his men to keep fighting, even though it seemed that U.S. troops would surely lose. As he was talking to his men, a Mexican cannonball passed between his legs. Still Jackson held his ground.

Jackson's bravery and leadership were noticed by his commanding officers. In less than a year, he was promoted twice. By the end of the war, in 1848, Jackson had risen to the rank of brevet major, a temporary promotion given during battle.

Stonewall Jackson as a young lieutenant in the U.S. Army during the Mexican War

After the war, Jackson was assigned to Fort Hamilton, a few miles from New York City. The young man often traveled to the big, bustling city to shop at bookstores and read at public libraries. He also studied the Bible every day and attended a variety of churches, trying to decide which one was right for him. In his spare time, he enjoyed parties and sleigh rides with other

Fort Hamilton in Brooklyn, New York, overlooked New York Harbor and Staten Island.

young people in the area.

In 1850, Jackson's company was sent to Fort Meade in central Florida. Jackson quickly became bored working in the hot, swampy conditions. After all, he had been used to the excitement of battles in Mexico and the culture of New York. Jackson also disliked his commander, Captain William French, who criticized him and took away some of his responsibilities. When Jackson heard that French was mistreating his wife, he began investigating the rumors. In turn, French had Jackson arrested in April 1851. Jackson spent more than a month in jail.

Four days after Jackson was released, he resigned from the Army to teach philosophy at Virginia Military Institute (VMI) in Lexington, Virginia. VMI educated and prepared young men for military service.

Jackson's students, however, thought he was strict, boring, and serious, and they strongly disliked him. The cadets nicknamed him "Old Jack," "Tom Fool," and "Square Box," a jest about his big feet. One group of former students tried to have Jackson fired. Another student challenged him to a duel.

During his 10 years in Lexington, Jackson became quite religious. He joined a local church and vowed not to drink, smoke, or gamble. He also refused to do anything on Sundays—he wouldn't work, write letters, or read the newspaper.

Elinor "Ellie" Junkin (1825–1854) was Jackson's first wife.

While in Lexington, Jackson fell in love with a young woman named Elinor Junkin. The couple married in the summer of 1853, but their time together was short. Just 14 months after their marriage, Ellie died giving birth to their son, who was not alive when he was born.

Three years later, in 1857, Jackson married Mary Anna Morrison, the daughter of a Presbyterian minister from North Carolina. Together they enjoyed a happy home life, sometimes dancing the polka and play acting with each other. In April 1858, their first child, a daughter, was born. However, little Mary lived less than a month. The couple would have another daughter, Julia Laura, four years later in November 1862. But her father would be fighting in the Civil War when she was born.

Mary Anna Morrison (1831–1915)

4 Protecting Virginia

*I*n 1859, Thomas Jackson and 21 of his VMI cadets were ordered to report for duty in Charlestown, Virginia. Their assignment was to guard John Brown, an abolitionist whose radical fight against slavery had gotten him arrested. His attempt to start a rebellion of slaves at Harpers Ferry had failed, and he was captured and sentenced to death by hanging.

The following year, in 1860, Abraham Lincoln was

John Brown was sentenced to death for treason and inciting a slave rebellion.

elected president of the United States. People living in the South were afraid that Lincoln would try to end slavery. Most of them believed slavery was a necessary part of the Southern economy. Jackson was used to slavery and had grown up working side-by-side with his uncle's slaves. He also owned two slaves, and his wife owned four.

After Lincoln's election, South Carolina was the first state to secede from the United States. Jackson's home state of Virginia was the eighth. Eleven states eventually left the Union and became a new country—the Confederate

Abraham Lincoln (1809–1865) was the 16th president of the United States.

Jackson eventually reached the rank of lieutenant general in the Confederate Army.

States of America. Jefferson Davis was its president.

Jackson didn't think the North and South should split. He believed the two sides should try to solve their problems together. But when Virginia seceded, Jackson had to choose between his country and his state. Almost immediately, he decided to remain loyal to Virginia. Four days later, he was named a colonel in Virginia's army.

On July 21, Jackson fought in the first major battle of the Civil War. The Battle of First Manassas began when Union troops attacked Confederate soldiers at Manassas Junction. Northerners were so certain of victory that spectators made the 30-mile (48-kilometer) trip from Washington, D.C., to watch the South be defeated. Men and women clad in fine clothes stood on a nearby hill, watching the battle as if it were a play.

As the Union pushed Southern soldiers back, it looked like the Northern army would win the day—and put a swift end to the war. But Jackson was not ready to surrender. Even though he had been shot in the finger, he stayed with his men, telling them, "Steady, men, steady! All's well!" His presence encouraged fleeing Southern soldiers to come back and fight. Southern troops compared his firm stand to a stone wall.

By the end of the day, the Union Army was on the run.

The First Battle of Manassas, also called Bull Run

The Confederates had defeated the North, but both sides had suffered terrible casualties. About 2,000 Confederate troops died, and 3,000 Union soldiers were killed. Many more were wounded, captured, or missing.

Southerners praised Jackson and his men for the victory. Jackson became known simply as Stonewall, and his men were called the Stonewall Brigade. For his efforts, Jackson was promoted to the rank of major general.

5 The Shenandoah Valley

After Bull Run, Stonewall Jackson was sent to defend Virginia's Shenandoah Valley. The region with its rich farmland was important to the Confederacy since much of the food for the Confederate Army came from the area. It was also important to the Union. If they captured the Shenandoah Valley, the Confederates would have no food supply and would be forced to surrender. The Valley was also a perfect avenue to the North, and the region became a target.

During the winter of 1861–1862, Jackson and his men saw little action in the Valley. The quiet break was a perfect opportunity for Jackson's wife to visit him in Winchester. Anna stayed near the Confederate camp for nearly two months.

In early March 1862, Jackson sent Anna back home. Pleasant weather had returned, and he knew the quiet wouldn't

Jackson's Confederate Army headquarters were in the city of Winchester.

last long. Jackson was right. Soon after Anna left, the Union

Army took control of Winchester.

Later that month, Jackson and his men began marching

toward Washington, D.C. Jackson didn't intend to attack the city.

Instead he hoped that Union troops marching toward Richmond,

Virginia, the capital of the Confederacy, would turn around to

pursue him. After the Battle of Kernstown on March 23, Union troops marching out of the Valley reversed course. Jackson's strategy was working. He held Union forces in the Valley for five more battles, kept them away from Richmond, and pushed them back toward Washington, D.C.

By the end of the Shenandoah Valley campaign in June,

Jackson's decisive victory at the two-day Battle of Front Royal, Virginia, caused Union soldiers to retreat and brought an end to the Shenandoah Valley campaign.

Jackson had fought six battles. He had also initiated a dozen strategies that delayed or held back Union troops. Jackson explained his strategy to General John D. Imboden: "Always mystify, mislead, and surprise the enemy, if possible. And when you strike and overcome him, never give up the pursuit as long as your men have the strength to follow."

About 7,000 Northern soldiers died during the Shenandoah Valley campaign; Southern troops suffered about half as many losses. Jackson's soldiers seized much-needed weapons and supplies from retreating Union troops, who headed back to Washington, D.C.

6

Triumph

*S*tonewall Jackson's fame spread all over the South. He quickly became a Confederate hero and legend. In the North, he became one of the most hated and feared of all the Confederate commanders.

General Robert E. Lee, commander in chief of the Confederate Army, ordered Jackson to come to Richmond with his troops. Lee needed Jackson's help to fight off part of the Union

Like Jackson, General Robert E. Lee chose to remain loyal to Virginia and fight for the South.

29

Army near the Confederate capital.

Major General Jackson and his men marched quickly toward Richmond. They were known to cover as many as 40 miles (64 km) on foot in one day—as far as a man on horseback would typically travel in a day. Jackson's soldiers thus became known as foot cavalry. Jackson arrived at Richmond in late June, and by the end of a week, the South had driven Union General George B. McClellan from the area.

After the victory, confident Confederate soldiers fought in battle after battle. Then Jackson and his 14,000 troops headed north to attack Maryland. On the way, Jackson captured Harpers Ferry, where the Union Army had camped. More than 12,500 Union soldiers were taken prisoner, the highest number captured during the Civil War.

On September 17, 1862, Jackson led his troops north across the Potomac River to Sharpsburg, Maryland. Jackson

In September 1862, the Confederate Army crossed the Potomac River into Maryland at White's Ford, the South's first invasion of the North.

arrived just in time to save Lee's forces from being wiped out.

Known in the North as the Battle of Antietam, the battle at

Sharpsburg was the bloodiest and most deadly day of the entire

war. It was also the first major Civil War battle on Northern soil.

By the time the battle ended, nearly 13,000 Union soldiers were

The Battle of Antietam, also known as the Battle of Sharpsburg, was the first major battle of the Civil War to be fought on Northern soil.

dead, wounded, or missing. The Confederates lost 10,000 soldiers and were forced out of Maryland and back into Virginia.

After the Battle of Antietam, there was quiet for two months. Back on Southern soil, Jackson and his men waited, and on December 11, the Battle of Fredericksburg began. The Union had 120,000 troops, while Lee had less than 80,000. Not only were the Southern troops outnumbered, they were also

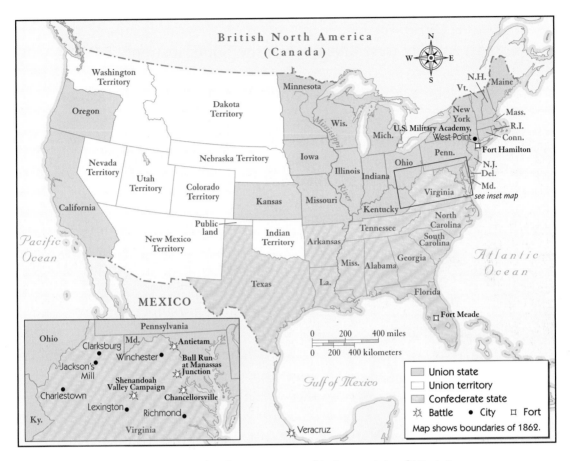

Jackson spent most of his life and military career in his home state of Virginia.

out-classed. Confederate General James Longstreet described the difference: "Jackson's ragged infantry ... [was] a striking contrast to the handsomely equipped troops of the Federals [North]." But despite their shortcomings, Lee and Jackson managed to defeat the huge Union force. That day more than 12,500

Northern soldiers were killed, while the South lost only 5,000 troops. Jackson's reputation as an extraordinary military leader grew. And victory after victory convinced Southerners that the Confederacy could win the war.

In April 1863, Lee and Jackson moved their men to Chancellorsville, Virginia. Later that month, Jackson allowed his wife and 5-month-old Julia to visit. But their time together was cut short when Jackson learned that Northern soldiers were nearby.

Julia, the only Jackson child to survive infancy, was born in November 1862.

7 Tragedy

On May 1, 1863, the Battle of Chancellorsville began. Even though the Union Army outnumbered the Confederates by nearly two to one, Stonewall Jackson was ready. The second day of battle, Jackson and his men attacked from the rear.

Union troops fled, surprised by the rear assault. The Battle of Chancellorsville became known as Lee's greatest victory, but Lee's success was due in large part to Jackson.

Toward the

Generals Robert E. Lee and Stonewall Jackson conferred before the Battle of Chancellorsville in 1863.

end of the day, Jackson rode out to the front lines to watch the Union soldiers flee and to plan another attack. The night sky darkened, and Jackson and some of his officers headed back to camp behind the battle line. As they neared Confederate lines, disaster struck. Nervous Confederate guards mistook Jackson and his officers for Northern spies and began firing at them.

Two of Jackson's men were shot dead. Jackson tried to escape the rain of bullets, but he was hit three times. One bullet hit his upper left arm, seriously injuring him just below the shoulder. Another bullet went through his left forearm; and yet another bullet struck the palm of his right hand. Jackson fell from his horse to the ground.

Confederate soldiers carried Jackson to the medical tent where doctors examined his wounds. They believed the famous commander would survive if they amputated his left arm. Jackson agreed. After making their patient unconscious, a

Unable to identify Jackson in the twilight, Confederate soldiers fired at their own general.

surgeon amputated Jackson's arm about 2 inches (5 centimeters) below his shoulder.

When General Lee heard about Jackson's wounds, he ordered the injured officer to be taken to Guiney Station, 27 miles

(43 km) from the battlefield. Lee believed Jackson would be safe there from enemy fire. On the way to the railway station, men and women flocked to Jackson's side, giving him food and trying to lift his spirits.

At first, Jackson seemed to be healing well. Then five days after his operation, he came down with pneumonia. He was so sick that his wife and daughter were called to his side. Anna sang hymns to comfort him, but he continued to get worse.

On Sunday May 10, 1863, eight days after he was shot, Thomas "Stonewall" Jackson died. He was 39 years old. At his funeral, 20,000 people filed by the commander's coffin to pay their last respects to one of the greatest military leaders the nation had ever seen. Jackson's coffin was wrapped in a Confederate flag.

Jackson's life and military service had encouraged and inspired Southerners. Now many of them believed the

A monument adorned with Confederate flags marks the grave of Thomas "Stonewall" Jackson in Lexington, Virginia.

Confederacy couldn't win the war without him. In July 1863, the North and the South fought their deadliest battle—the three-day Battle of Gettysburg. The Confederate Army could have used Jackson's courage and tactical strategies in what was called the turning point of the war.

The Civil War finally came to an end April 9, 1865, when General Lee surrendered to Union General Ulysses S. Grant at Appomattox Court House, Virginia.

Thomas "Stonewall" Jackson is still honored in the South. Statues throughout Virginia memorialize this fallen hero of the Confederacy. Lee-Jackson Day, a Virginia state holiday, serves as a yearly reminder of the birthdays of both Robert E. Lee and Thomas "Stonewall" Jackson.

In New York, West Point Academy still teaches Jackson's strategies and battle tactics to young Army cadets. Although he was a Southern general, Jackson became a symbol of determina-

A bronze statue of Thomas "Stonewall" Jackson outside Virginia Military Institute depicts the general surveying his troops before the Battle of Chancellorsville.

tion and bravery for Americans everywhere. Thomas "Stonewall" Jackson, the man who was adored by his troops and feared by his enemies, has made his mark on history as one of the great generals of the Civil War.

Glossary

abolitionist—person who favors ending slavery

brevet—battlefield promotion, without additional pay, that can later become permanent

cadet—student at a military school who is training to be an officer

campaign—set of military operations aimed at achieving a goal

casualties—those injured, killed, captured, or missing in action during a battle

company—army unit under command of a captain

Confederacy—Southern states that fought against Northern states in the Civil War; also called the Confederate States of America

duel—formal fight between two people, usually with guns or swords, used to settle an argument

pneumonia—disease marked by inflammation of the lungs

regiment—military unit made up of 1,000 to 3,000 soldiers

secede—to formally withdraw from an organization, state, or country

Union—Northern states that fought against Southern states in the Civil War

Did You Know?

- Stonewall Jackson's 1st Brigade was made up of men from all walks of life: farmers, blacksmiths, carpenters, clerks, "gentlemen," and students from a theology school. The students named their cannons Matthew, Mark, Luke, and John, after the authors of the four gospels of the New Testament of the Bible.

- During the war, Jackson's sister Laura cared for wounded Union soldiers in her home. Because she aided the enemy, Jackson and his sister never spoke or wrote to each other again.

- When Jackson's horse, Little Sorrel, died, his stuffed hide was put on display at Virginia Military Institute.

- The Battle of Antietam was the bloodiest day in the Civil War. President Lincoln felt that the Union victory gave him enough authority to sign the Emancipation Proclamation, declaring all slaves in the Confederate states free.

- Jackson's amputated left arm was buried in an unmarked grave in Ellwood Cemetery in Spotsylvania, Virginia. Forty years later, in 1903, a simple granite marker was placed at the burial site. It reads, "Arm of Stonewall Jackson, May 3, 1863."

- A huge sculpture of Stonewall Jackson on his horse is carved into the side of Stone Mountain near Atlanta, Georgia. The gigantic work of art, which covers about 3 acres (1.2 hectares), also shows Robert E. Lee and Jefferson Davis on horseback.

Important Dates

Timeline

1824	Born January 21 in Clarksburg, West Virginia
1846	Graduates from the U.S. Military Academy and begins a career in the U.S. Army
1851	Resigns from the Army to teach at Virginia Military Institute
1853	Marries Elinor "Ellie" Junkin
1854	Ellie dies while giving birth to their stillborn son
1857	Marries Mary Anna Morrison
1858	Daughter Mary dies shortly after birth
1859	Guards abolitionist John Brown prior to Brown's execution
1861	Virginia secedes from the Union on April 17; Jackson chooses to fight for the new Confederate States of America; in July, First Battle of Bull Run earns Jackson the nickname "Stonewall"
1862	Begins Shenandoah Valley campaign; daughter Julia is born in November
1863	Shot accidentally by his own troops; his arm is amputated; dies May 10 at the age of 39

Important People

John Brown (1800–1859)
Abolitionist who tried to start a slave rebellion at Harpers Ferry, West Virginia, in 1859; he failed and was tried for the murder of five Southerners, inciting a rebellion, and treason against the state of Virginia; he was hanged by the U.S. government

Robert E. Lee (1807–1870)
Commander of the Confederate Army during the Civil War; considered Jackson to be his most brilliant general and his "right arm"; surrendered to Union commander Ulysses S. Grant at Appomattox Court House, Virginia, on April 9, 1865; after the war he encouraged reconciliation between the North and the South

Abraham Lincoln (1809–1865)
President of the United States during the Civil War; after his election in 1860, Southern states began seceding from the Union, fearing that Lincoln would put an end to slavery; assassinated shortly after General Lee surrendered and the Civil War came to an end

Mary Anna Morrison (1831–1915)
Second wife of Stonewall Jackson; after her husband's death, she kept his memory alive by encouraging those who knew Jackson to write about him; she later penned her own book about his life and career; she never remarried and became known as the Widow of the Confederacy

Want to Know More?

More Books to Read

Brager, Bruce L. *There He Stands: The Story of Stonewall Jackson*. Greensboro, N.C.: Morgan Reynolds Publishing, Inc., 2004.

Burgan, Michael. *The Assassination of Abraham Lincoln*. Minneapolis: Compass Point Books, 2005.

Gillis, Jennifer B. *The Confederate Soldier*. Minneapolis: Compass Point Books, 2007.

McPherson, James M. *Fields of Fury: The American Civil War*. New York: Atheneum Books for Young Readers, 2002.

Robertson, James I. *Standing Like a Stone Wall: The Life of General Thomas J. Jackson*. New York: Atheneum, 2001.

On the Web

For more information on this topic, use FactHound.

1. Go to *www.facthound.com*

2. Choose your grade level.

3. Begin your search.

This book's ID number is 9780756541101

FactHound will find the best sites for you.

On the Road

Fredericksburg and Spotsylvania National Military Park
120 Chatham Lane
Fredericksburg, VA 22405–2508
540/373-4510
A military park that stands where some of the bloodiest battles of the Civil War were waged

Stonewall Jackson Museum
33229 Old Valley Pike
Strasburg, VA 22657
540/465-5884
Features information about the Civil War and Stonewall Jackson, the famous Confederate Civil War commander

Look for more We the People Biographies:

American Patriot: Benjamin Franklin

Civil War Spy: Elizabeth Van Lew

Confederate Commander: General Robert E. Lee

First of First Ladies: Martha Washington

A Signer for Independence: John Hancock

Soldier and Founder: Alexander Hamilton

Union General and 18th President: Ulysses S. Grant

A complete list of We the People titles is available on our Web site:
www.compasspointbooks.com

Index

About the Author

Robin S. Doak has been writing for children for more than 16 years. A former editor of *Weekly Reader* and *U*S*Kids* magazines, Doak has authored fun and educational materials for kids of all ages. She is a past winner of the Educational Press Association of America Distinguished Achievement Award. She lives with her husband in Maine.